DAY TRADING

OPTIONS

THE FIRST INVESTORS GUIDE TO KNOW THE
SECRETS OF OPTIONS FOR BEGINNERS. LEARN
TRADING BASICS TO INCREASE YOUR EARNINGS
AND ACQUIRE THE RIGHT MINDSET FOR
INVESTING.

ANDREW ELDER

original author of this work can be in any fashion deemed liable for any hardship or damages that may befall them after undertaking the information described herein.

Additionally, the information in the following pages is intended only for informational purposes and should thus be thought of as universal. As befitting its nature, it is presented without assurance regarding its prolonged validity or interim quality. Trademarks that are mentioned are done without written consent and can in no way be considered an endorsement from the trademark holder.

TABLE OF CONTENT

Introduction

Before you dive into day trading, it helps to know a little bit about what it is and isn't. This is not investing, which means you buy a stake in an asset that you hold onto hope it will build a profit over some time. The amount of time you hold on to it depends on you. Most of the time, an investor will hold it for many years, even decades. They also look at the type of business they are investing in. They investigate the companies to make sure they stay away from litigation, have good products, keep debts paid, and make good profits.

Day trading is the opposite of this. It means that you buy and sell stocks in one day. Day traders can use their own or borrowed money to invest in stocks and make profits off small price changes in highly liquid stocks. They still follow the wisdom of long-term investors: buy low, sell high. Day traders simply do this in a shorter amount of time.

A typical day for a trader will look a little like this. At 10 AM the trade chooses to buy 1,000 shares of a certain stock. When it starts to rise at 10:15, they sell the stock. If it had risen by half when they sold it, they made a $500 profit, minus commission. Assuming the trader uses Scottrade; commission could be anywhere from $7 to $27, which means their profit would be around $493 to $473. Then they also have to consider their taxes. When a stock has been held for less than a year, taxes will be based on your gain rate, and this may be as high as 35%. Investments are typically taxed no higher than 20%. This means tax planning should be an important part of your day.

If the profit looks small to you, remember, day traders make many trades throughout the day, often upwards of 25 to 30. This means profits are multiplied by high trade volume. To cut back on risks, they don't keep stocks overnight because a lot can change in that time. Announcements by the corporation and events can increase the market volatility, so a trader has to be available and can respond quickly. As opposed to long-term investors that will wait and think through things and look at information, day traders will act quickly and decide on things a few minutes or even seconds.

There are also some other types of trading options that lie between these extremes. You have swing trading, in which you hold onto stocks for a couple of days. There is position trading, which means you hold onto stocks for weeks or months. They all have their risks, and day trading tends to be the riskiest and most controversial.

History

The popularity of day trading is still fairly new. Different events and rulings over the past 100 years made day trading what it is. The following are the most important things that have happened in the day trading career that has made it so popular.

Traders used the first ticker tape in 1867, which meant it was easier for them to communicate information on transactions that took place on the exchange. Most brokers that traded on the Stock Exchange in New York kept close offices so they could get a regular tape feed.

At the height of one of the most popular bull markets, in 1928, traders couldn't access direct markets. This meant they had to use a broker to place an order from the information on ticker tapes.

The NASDAQ was created in 1971 by the NASD.

In 1975, the SEC came up with new rules which got rid of fixed commissions. This was the first time in more than 180 years that the market competition would set the trading fees. A lot of firms, including Charles Schwab, began giving clients discount rates for trades. This began the discount brokerage era.

In 1987, the majority of trades were done over the phone. This enabled the firms that bought and sold NASDAQ to avoid small investors that would try and call in trades during the crash in October. The SEC responded to this problem by creating the SOES, which is the small order entry system, which gave 1,000 shares or fewer priority.

At the dot-com craze height in 1997, people began to view technology stocks as a bull market. This was also a time where the internet started to become easier to use for everybody. Many of the current trading companies made their first websites. This helped small traders have access to price quotes and activities, which helped to provide everybody with a level playing field.

The attention to day trading continued to grow in 1999. The SEC chairman, Arthur Levitt, testified to Congress that he had estimated the number of day traders was around 7,000.

He also said that the number of investors that used the internet was around 5 million. During this time, negative headlines about day trading began to circle.

One of the negative headlines was when Mark Barton shot up a day trading office in Atlanta. This made people think that day trading was way too stressful. Then two weeks later, the North American Securities Administrators Association came out with a statement that said seven out of ten-day traders would end up losing all of their money.

In 2000, changes to the SOES were made to get rid of advantages for day traders, but then a stock market collapse came. After the dot-com bubble burst, many day traders became frightened or bankrupt and ran to different careers. The crazy frontier ways of day trading came to an end in 2008, as well as people who hope to get rich quickly. Now there are more professional day traders that work with diligence and care as if it were any other job.

Take a step towards day trading

In theory, anybody could be a pro football player, but in reality, there are a few people that have the right skill set for that sport. The same goes for day traders. The best traders need to have certain traits and have certain resources for them to be successful. Here are some of the most important things:

- Market knowledge and experience – To be successful with day trading, you are going to have to have some knowledge of market fundamentals. The most successful day traders are people who have experience in investing and in trading. They also make sure that they research things before they jump in.

- Capital – It may seem like a cliché, but "It takes money to make money," and this is extremely true when talking about day traders. A lot of traders will choose to borrow money, known as leverage, that they use to make their trades. Leverage tends to be riskier. Others make sure they have their capital saved before they trade.

- Business plan – When you choose to start day trading, you become a business owner, and this means you need a business plan. This plan should address your long and short-term goals, target markets, metrics, trading days and hours, reporting, business needs, tax considerations, and capital investment

- Discipline – Day traders have to avoid buying and selling based on their emotions. They understand how they should work with risk capital, they make sure they follow their limit and stop orders, to keep losses low, and they close out at the end of every business day.

- Technology – Day trading has to be done through electronic communication networks. You have to have use of a high-speed connection and a reliable computer to access the internet. A lot of traders will use a PC that has control over two monitors, a Wi-Fi connection on a laptop, a DSL backup, a clone computer, and cable broadband. They also have analytical software to control their accounts, research trades, perform trades, and receive information.

If a person decides to start day trading without having access to the necessary resources, they will most likely fail. If they do end up succeeding, they will most likely encounter a large learning curve. Once they gain experience, traders will either end up becoming a professional with an institution, or they will work by themselves. Either way, it is a full-time commitment.

Trading Secrets

As hard as day trading may seem, it becomes a lot easier once you learn a few rules and strategies about the way the market moves. Here are ten secrets that will help you to become a better day trader.

1. **Only trade with money you can afford to lose.**

A great trader will make sure to set aside some risk capital and will set aside a lot of money for long-term goals and retirement. Larger amounts of money should be invested for longer durations and in a more conservative fashion. It's not forbidden to use it when day trading, but you have to make sure that you have very favorable odds.

2. Don't risk a large amount of capital on a single trade.

Every day you should take the time to set a certain amount of your daily budget for each trade you plan on making. This is going to depend on the amount of money you have set aside to invest. Otherwise, you could end up missing out on some great opportunities.

3. Never Limit Yourself to Just Stocks.

Futures, options, and Forex are all asset options that will provide you with volatility and liquidity just like stocks will, which means they are great for day trading. A lot of the time, one of these options is going to give you an appealing opportunity when the stock market isn't doing very well.

4. Learn from previous experiences, but never second-guess yourself

Every day trader is going to experience a loss, so don't get upset with yourself when a trade ends up not working the way you thought it would. All you have to do is make sure you follow all of your rules and make sure you make no mistakes.

5. Keep an eye out for imbalanced supply and demand.

Like all things in life, if the supply is almost exhausted, and there are a lot of buyers, the price is going to end up going up. If there is a lot of supply, but not enough buyers that are interested, the price is going to go down.

6. **Have a target price before you start your day**.

Before you start to buy a stock, figure what profit is the most acceptable and then a stop-loss if your trade starts to go south. You have to stick to these choices once you make them. This will make sure you don't become greedy and will, more importantly, limit losses.

6. **Set a risk-reward ratio of 3:1 once you set targets.**

One of the most important things is to make sure you have a good risk-reward ratio. This will make sure that you receive big wins and small losses.

CHAPTER 1:

What Is Options Trading?

There are two significant ways you can trade options. The first involves buying the option itself and speculating on the price of the premium. The price of the premium is going to fluctuate based on how the underlying stock moves so you can profit from these movements. For example, if you think a stock is going to go up, you can buy an in-the-money call, and as the stock rises, the intrinsic value increases as well.

Thus, you benefit from the rise in the overall premium value. With a put, as the stock falls, the intrinsic value of the put rises, and so does its premium. Remember, you're buying a put to benefit from the price drop (you're not selling a put). The second method of speculating in options is not to pay as much attention to the premium but to the underlying.

What I mean is that you're not concerned with the price rise in the underlying, you're far more concerned with exercising the option. This involves an additional step, but if you aim to own the stock, then this could be a better method for you to deploy. Generally speaking, a lot of options traders don't bother exercising the contract since the premium tends to capture the intrinsic value change pretty well.

Pretty straightforward so far, isn't it? You can swing or day trade options like common stock, but these methods will need you to develop a directional bias in the markets. As we've seen, this increases your risk and is no different from usual trading activity. The point is, you don't need options to trade this way. So how does one trade option intelligently?

Well, the best method to do this is to use the structure of the contracts themselves to isolate yourself from major market risk factors such as volatility. Often when swing or day trading, traders will use what is called a stop-loss order to limit their downside. This is a safety net only on paper since the market is liable to simply jump the stop loss level during times of high volatility.

So, the trader is faced with larger than expected losses, and in some cases, such volatility might wipe out their entire account as well. Options avoid all this drama since you will only pay the premium upfront, thereby limiting your initial investment greatly. Then, you will be using ironclad contracts to protect your downside, and therefore, there is no possibility of the market jumping the price. Even if it does, your contract specifies the price, so you will always receive the price as stated on it.

The Risks of Options Trading

Thus far, I've only been mentioning the trading of options concerning the underlying stock's movements. If you think it's going to rise, you buy a call. If you think it's going to fall, buy a put. Well, can you short call or a put? Yes, you can, and this is precisely where the risks inherent to options trading enter the picture.

When you buy an options contract, your risk is limited to the terms of the contract. The person who sold you the contract receives the premium in exchange for selling it to you. They keep this premium no matter what. The seller of the option is generally called the writer.

Option writing has its advantages. For one, the majority of options traded tend to expire out of the money. Hence, the writer keeps the premium on the option and usually doesn't have to worry about the contract being exercised. If the contract does get exercised, this leads to a whole world of trouble. Think about this scenario: if you've written a call (that is, sold it), and if it moves into the money, your downside is unlimited.

Remember that when you're writing a call, you're betting that the underlying stock will not rise. Well, if it does arise, it can rise to infinite levels. What if your call's strike price is at $10 and before the expiry date, the stock rises to $10,000? Unlikely, I know, but theoretically possible.

The loss will easily exceed your account's equity.

Writing a put doesn't have an unlimited downside, but it does have a large one, nonetheless. If the strike price of the put you wrote is at $50, your downside is a total of $50 per share (since the stock can decline only till 0). This is why writing options need to be carried out carefully.

So, if the risks are this huge, why do people write options in the first place? Well, aside from the fact that option writing usually results in a profit (via earning the premium), most option writers cover their downside by covering their option positions. So, if someone writes a call, they buy the underlying stock first. Another option is to buy a put at a lower strike price since this covers their downside.

You must understand the differences between writing options naked and writing them when covered. Naked option writing is the riskiest thing that you can do, and in fact, your broker will not allow you to do this. Covered writing is perfectly fine, and no broker is going to stop you from doing this.

In case you're wondering, once you write an option, you can buy it back at a lower price before the expiry date. In other words, you can short an option like you would a stock. Generally, with the strategies, you won't need to do this unless you adjust your trades.

Options have leverage inherent in them, and you should be

aware of this fact. Every contract represents control over 100 shares of the underlying stock, so everything that happens is magnified by a 100x multiple. This makes it even more crucial that you execute your strategies perfectly.

Other than this, options don't present any risks. They reduce your risk of trading in the market thanks to minimizing the effects of volatility. Volatility is both a blessing and a curse for directional traders. On the one hand, it makes them money via massive swings. However, it's not so much fun when the swings go the other way and wipe them out.

Options Trading Accounts

To trade options, you will need to open a brokerage account. At this point, you have a choice. You can either go with a full-service broker or a discount broker. A full-service broker is an institution that is like a financial supermarket. They have financial advisors on their payroll and can help you with stuff like retirement planning, tax planning, and so on.

A full-service house will also have its line of ETFs and mutual funds, which you can invest in. People generally open their retirement accounts with full-service brokers since it gives them a feeling of greater security. However, this is a false impression. The markets in the United States are extremely well regulated, no matter what the doomsday experts tell you. You don't face lesser risks with a full-service broker than you would anywhere else. Full-service brokers charge higher commissions, and the only advantage of such an institution is that connecting your various accounts becomes easier. If someone has a retirement account with one firm, inertia leads them to open another with the same institution, much like how people usually stick to the same bank for their entire lives (Pritchard, 2019).

A mistake that people make when choosing full-service brokers are to think that they'll receive trading advice. Get this clear: your broker has zero obligation to provide you with advice. Their fiduciary duty extends only as far as executing your trades as best as possible. Your broker isn't there to tell you which stock is going to go up or which is the best stock for your retirement account.

Sure, they might have an army of CFAs in-house, but these employees are not allowed to recommend outside ETFs and products to their clients. The in-house funds always have a higher fee attached to them. So, there's a huge conflict of interest there. My point is, don't blindly trust your broker, especially if they have CFAs on their payroll. They don't provide unbiased investment advice, so why would they ever give you trading advice?

Generally speaking, remember that your broker is not your friend. This is not to say they're your enemy, but they have a certain function in the market, and their job is to execute that. It isn't to do anything else. It's a bit like going to the florist and asking for bread. The fault isn't with them; it's with those who expect the wrong things from their broker.

This brings me to discount brokers. Discount brokerage houses are all about trimming the fat and will offer you one thing only: execution. As a result, you'll pay far lower commissions. Transaction costs are extremely important when it comes to trading. Traders usually think that buying and selling in the market is a zero-sum game. If someone wins an amount, someone else loses that same amount.

This is not true. The broker makes money no matter what

happens in the market. Your transaction costs form a hurdle that you must jump to profit. Consider this example: let's say your broker charges you 0.1% per trade. So, when you buy, you pay 0.1%, and when you sell, you pay 0.1%. Remember, this is whether you win or lose.

So, every trade needs to make at least 0.21% to profit. It doesn't sound like much. However, if you place 100 trades per year, this means you need to make 20% just to breakeven (0.2*100). Most days, traders place 100 trades per month! So over time, you can see how this hurdle rate adds up massively. This is why you should include your commissions in all your profit and loss calculations. If you choose to risk a certain percentage of your account on a trade, you need to factor in the commission costs on the gain or loss amount. Both directional and options traders need to follow this advice, although the impact is reduced quite a bit for option traders. Discount brokers' fees will vary depending on the type of trader they're geared towards. Platforms that are beginner-appropriate will have fees per leg or a fixed fee, which is on a per-share basis plus an additional fee since it involves an option transaction. Make sure you differentiate between the per share fees and the fees for a contract.

Some brokers quote prices for a contract while some quote it per leg and so on. There's no standardized method here. Simply go for the lowest price and the best platform.

This invariably happens to result in traders choosing Interactive Brokers. Lightspeed is another great platform, but this is aimed at more advanced and very active options traders so that I wouldn't recommend this for beginners.

CHAPTER 2:

Understand and Manage Risk

E ffectively managing your capital and hazard presentation is essential when exchanging choices. While hazard is unavoidable with a venture, your introduction to chance shouldn't be an issue. The key is to manage the hazard reserves reasonably; continually guarantee that you approve of the degree of hazard being taken and that you are not presenting yourself to nonsensical misfortunes.

Comparable thoughts can be applied while managing your cash also. You should exchange using capital that you can stand to lose; swear off overstretching yourself. As powerful cash and hazard the board are crucial to productive alternatives exchanging, it's a subject that you genuinely need to appreciate. We will investigate a part of the methods you can, and should, use for controlling your financial plan and dealing with your hazard presentation.

- Managing Risk with Options Spreads
- Managing Risk Using Options Orders
- Managing Risk through Diversification
- Using Your Trading Plan
- Money Management and Position Sizing

Utilizing Your Trading Plan

It's basic to have a quick and dirty exchanging plan that spreads out guidelines and boundaries for your exchanging works out. One of the businesslike employments of such an arrangement is to help you in managing your cash and your hazard introduction. Your arrangement should join subtleties of what level of hazard you approve of and the measure of capital you have to use.

By following your arrangement and simply using the cash that you have expressly circulated for choices exchanging, you can avoid most likely the best mistake that merchants and financial specialists make: using "frightened" cash.

At the point when you are exchanging with cash that you either cannot stand to lose or should have put something aside for different purposes, you are far less slanted to choose objective decisions in your trades. While it's difficult to evacuate the feeling engaged with choices exchanging, you genuinely need to be as based as possible on what you are doing and why.

At the point when feeling accept authority over, you

potentially start to lose your focus and are committed to acting unreasonably. It may make you seek after misfortunes from past exchanges that went bad, for example, or making exchanges that you wouldn't by and large make. On the off chance that you follow your arrangement and stick to using your speculation capital, at that point you ought to have a significantly improved potential for the accomplishment of checking your feelings.

So also, you should adhere to the degrees of hazard that you outline in your arrangement. If you need to make generally safe exchanges, by then there is no purpose for why you should start presenting yourself to increasingly raised degrees of hazard. It's much of the time alluring to do this, perhaps because you have made two or three misfortunes and you have to endeavor to fix them, or conceivably you have done well with some okay exchanges and need to start extending your benefits at a speedier rate.

Overseeing Risk with Options Spreads

Alternatives spreads are considerable and basic devices in choice exchanging. A choice spread is basically when you join more than one situation on alternatives contracts reliant on similar basic security to reasonably make one in general exchanging position.

For example, if you bought in the cash approaches a specific stock and, at that point composed more affordable out of the cash approaches a similar stock, by then, you would have made a spread known as a bull call spread. Buying the calls infers you remain to get if the concealed stock goes up in esteem, anyway you would lose a couple or the aggregate of the cash spent to get them if the expense of the stock neglected to go up. By making approaches a similar stock you would have the choice to control a segment of the basic expenses and along these lines diminish the greatest measure of cash you could lose.

All choices exchanging techniques include the use of spreads, and these spreads speak to an important strategy to oversee hazards. This suggests you perhaps reduce the advantages you would make, anyway it decreases the general hazard.

Spreads can moreover be used to diminish the dangers included when entering a short position. For example, on the off chance that you wrote in the cash puts on stock, by then you would get a forthright installment for composing those choices, in any case, you would be presented to expected misfortunes if the stock dropped in esteem. On the off chance that you in like manner bought more affordable out of cash puts, at that point you would need to contribute a bit of your forthright installment, notwithstanding, you would top any potential misfortunes that a reduction in the stock would cause. This accurate sort of spread is known as a bull put spread.

As ought to be evident from both these models, it's conceivable to enter positions where you despite everything stand to pick up if the value moves the correct path for you, yet you can cautiously limit any misfortunes you may acquire if the value moves against you. This is the explanation spreads are so comprehensively used by choice dealers; they are mind-blowing gadgets for chance administration.

There is a tremendous extent of spreads that can be used to exploit or essentially any market circumstance.

Overseeing Risk Through Diversification

Enhancement is a hazard to the boarding procedure that is normally used by monetary experts that are building an arrangement of stocks by using a buy and hold method. The fundamental standard of broadening for such speculators is that spreading ventures over different associations and fragments cause a sensible portfolio instead of having a ton of cash tied up in one explicit association or area. A broadened portfolio is generally seen as less presented to chance than a portfolio that is made up by and large of one unequivocal kind of venture.

Concerning alternatives, expansion isn't huge in the same fantastic way; at any rate, it does at present have its uses and you can expand in different habits. Even though the

the way that the by and large proceeds as in the past, you needn't bother with a great deal of your capital submitted on one explicit sort of speculation, enhancement is used in choices exchanging through a grouping of strategies.

You can broaden by using a choice of different methodology, by exchanging choices that rely upon an extent of essential protections, and by exchanging different sorts of choices. Using development is that you stay to make benefits in different manners and you are not inside and out reliant on one explicit outcome for all of your exchanges to be fruitful.

Overseeing Risk Using Options Orders

A reasonably fundamental approach to oversee chance is to utilize the extent of different requests that you can put.

Likewise, the four major request types that you use to open and close circumstances, there is a portion of the additional requests that you can put, and an impressive parcel of these can assist you with chance administration.

For example, a normal market request will be filled at the best available cost at the hour of execution. This is a perfectly common way to deal with buy and sell choices, in any case, in an unpredictable market, your request may end up getting filled at a worth that is higher or lower than you need it to be. By using limit orders, where you can set the most extreme and least costs at which your request can be filled, you can keep away from buying or selling at less perfect costs.

There are orders that you can use to mechanize leaving a position: regardless of whether to bolt a benefit previously made or cut misfortunes on an exchange that didn't end up being admirable.

By using orders, for instance, the cutoff stop request, the trailing stop request, or the market stop request, you can without much of a stretch control what you leave a position.

This will help you with staying away from circumstances where you pass up benefits by clutching a situation for quite a while or bring about enormous misfortunes by not finishing off on an awful position quickly enough. By using alternative arranges reasonably, you can limit the hazard you are introduced to on every exchange you make.

Cash Management and Position Sizing

Dealing with your cash is indivisibly associated with overseeing hazards and both are likewise noteworthy. You, finally, have a restricted measure of cash to use, and because it's vital to keep tight control of your capital spending plan and to guarantee that you don't lose everything and get yourself unable to make extra exchanges.

Irrefutably the best way to deal with managing your cash is to use a truly basic thought known as position estimating. Position measuring is picking the measure of your capital you need to use to enter a particular position.

To reasonably use position measuring, you need to consider the amount to put resources into each exchange

terms of a level of your general venture capital.

In various respects, position measuring is a kind of enhancement. By simply using a little level of your capital in any one exchange, you will never be excessively reliant on one express outcome. Indeed, even the best merchants will make exchanges that turn out gravely; the key is to ensure the dreadful ones don't influence you harshly.

For example, if you have 50 percent of your speculation capital tied up in one exchange and it ends up losing you cash, at that point, you will have no doubt lost a

great deal of your accessible assets. If you

watch out for simply using 5% to 10% of your capital per exchange, by then even a few back-to-back losing exchanges shouldn't get you out.

On the off chance that you are certain that your exchanging plan will be compelling as time goes on, at that point, you ought to have the choice to cross the awful periods and still have enough cash-flow to get something going.

CHAPTER 3:

Software Needed Before Learning

What is MetaTrader 4 (MT4)?

MetaTrader 4, or MT4 for short, is a product that permits dealers to exchange outside trade and other budgetary items, for example, stocks, gold, oil, wares, lists, cryptos, and so on.

MT4 programming, created by MetaQuotes Software, Russia, was propelled in 2005. As of now, although numerous stages are being grown, even MT4's parent organization has propelled another exchanging stage, MT5, yet MT4 has consistently been the most well-known programming, utilized by numerous forex agents to offer types of assistance to their customers.

Step by step instructions to utilize MetaTrader 4

Every single fundamental component is situated in the main 3 bars of MT4. Fundamentally the principal bar will contain all the highlights, the subsequent bar contains the most much of the time utilized highlights. Also, the third bar centers around the element lines utilized for specialized investigation, for example, drawing trendlines, period outlines, notes...

Snap Views and you will see a table with essential highlights, the most significant of which is Market Watch (this rundown is generally left of course. On the off chance that your product doesn't show it, you simply need to press the console alternate route Ctrl + M to wrap up).

Images

The spot to show all cash sets you need to exchange with 3 primary things: Symbol, Bid, and Ask. Utilizing the correct mouse button on Symbol, you will see the accompanying table: New request, show all, Hide, Hide all, Chart window (there are numerous things however these are the most significant focuses you should know).

New request

This is utilized to enter another request, rapidly you simply need to utilize the console alternate way F9 to likewise show the request execution window as follows:

In this interface, when putting orders, you will take care of data about the request (Volume), stop misfortune (Stop Loss) and benefit (Take benefit). You cannot set Stop Loss or Take

Profit; however, you are required to fill in the exchange volume data.

Diagram Window

This is to open the diagram screen of the cash pair or item you have chosen when you right snap on it

Record

This shows the record you signed in to exchange.

Marker

The marker incorporates all the essential pointers that can be utilized for specialized examination, recognizing patterns in orders. In this area, you predominantly utilize two fundamental gatherings of pointers: the pattern marker (Trend) and the gathering of (Oscillators). Each piece of this segment will incorporate a wide range of pointers, to show all you simply need to tap on the + sign. To utilize a marker, right-click on the pointer and select "join to diagram".

Terminal (Ctrl + T)

This catch is for showing account (Balance), (Equity), and Margin at the current time and open or pending requests (on the off chance that you have an open or pending request).

Diagram

In this area, you have to think about the accompanying catches:

•   Candlesticks (easy route Alt + 2) are situated between the Line Chart and Bar Chart, are 3 regular diagrams in the monetary market. Be that as it may, in MT4, you should just utilize Candlesticks.

• Time Frame in MT4 exchanging programming: This territory comprises of catches M1, M5, M15, M30, H1, H4, D1, W1, and MN proportionate to periods of 1 moment, 5 minutes, 15 minutes, 30 minutes, 60 minutes, 4 hours, 1-day, multi-week and multi-month. Snap-on those catches to choose the period for showing the chart for investigation.

• Grid: lattice, shown in the graph isolated into little cells for a simple survey. On the off chance that you feel like the Grid needs to leave you to spot on click and select the Grid is finished.

• Properties: This catch is significant, helping you overhaul the MT4 graphical interface with the goal that it is anything but difficult to see and accommodates your style.

• Template: This catch is extremely valuable on the off chance that you have set up markers such as yourself, the diagrams of the sets you need to see the most, and you need to save this example for later exchanges. Simply click the Template button at that point Save Template and afterward name the chart format. If you need to use for whenever you simply need to return to the Template and select the layout by name will show up right away.

Investigate the Stocks to Work with

Before you bounce into the procedure of day exchanging, you

have to experience and do some exploration. There are likely a couple of stocks that, after some time, you will get increasingly acquainted with and choose are the correct one's for you to work with. You can go to and for between them, exchanging the one that bodes well for your requirements depending on how the market is going at that point. First and foremost, however, you should make an insincere effort and do a ton of examinations to see which stocks appear to be the best for you.

On the off chance that you have a specific methodology that you need to work with, this can be an incredible spot to begin. It will permit you an opportunity to experience and truly chip away at the stocks and search for the ones that are going to fit with this methodology and can assist you with getting the best outcomes here.

Once in a while, you may have a couple of techniques that we need to work with, and we can glance around and check whether any stocks are going to coordinate with these.

Remember that there will be a few days that work best with one sort of methodology, and afterward the following day, an alternate procedure will be the one that we work with. There is a great deal of unpredictability in the market, so we have to have some adaptability in what we do with day exchanging.

There will be a great deal of examination that accompanies this part. We should have the option to take a gander at a ton of diagrams and charts and find out about the long haul and the momentary patterns that accompany our stocks, and how we can use these for our necessities also. just when we have a decent comprehension of the patterns that accompany the stocks we need to utilize; at that point, we are prepared to enter an exchange.

CHAPTER 4:

Platform and Tools for option Trading

Before you begin with the alternatives exchanging that you need to do, it is imperative to stop and ensure that you know a portion of the terms. These terms are going to assist you with knowing increasingly about working in alternative exchanging, and can even assist you out if you decide to work in a couple of different markets too. We will likewise invest some energy discussing these terms all through this manual to assist you with a portion of the tips that we will discuss also. A portion of the terms that you should think about when you are prepared to begin with choices exchanging incorporate the Annual report.

This is a sort of report that an organization will get ready to intrigue their investors and uncover a great deal of money-related data. It contains a great deal of the data that you have to think about a specific organization before you put resources into them, regardless of whether it is stock exchanging, long haul or momentary exchanging, or alternatives exchanging. Ordinarily, it will discuss the obligation salary about the organization, its income, and even the administration procedure that it employs. At the point when you invest some energy perusing this yearly report, you ought to get a decent gander at the money-related circumstance and friends' dissolvability before you contribute. Exchange this is the way toward buying and afterward selling similar security, however on various markets, and regularly at various value focuses.

This can be utilized to assist you in getting more cash. You may locate that one alternative is accessible for $10 on the principal trade, yet then that equivalent choice is selling for $12 on another market. You would buy it from the main market and afterward sell on the subsequent one to make a benefit. Averaging down whenever that a speculator buys to a greater degree a stock as the value drops, is known as averaging down. This is going to make it with the goal that the normal value that you pay is going to diminish. You may wind up working with this procedure on the off chance that you accept that the accord that is out there concerning a specific organization isn't right, and you imagine that the cost is going to bounce back sometime in the not too distant future.

You could buy the choice as the cost goes down, taking it in at a decent cost, and afterward, when it bounces back, you will have the option to take those benefits. Bear advertise you will regularly find out about a bearish and a bullish market.

At the point when we talk about a bearish market, we are discussing when the market is experiencing a pattern of falling and the stock costs are going to travel south. If you notice that the cost of a stock begins to fall and

go down, it implies that it is bearish. Blue-chip stocks are the sort of stocks that you will discover behind a portion of the enormous, industry-driving organizations. They can offer you a steady record with higher profit installments, and they

as of now have developed notoriety of sound monetary administration. The articulation is thought to have originated from blue betting chips, which is the most elevated group of chips that you will see when betting in gambling

clubs. Positively trending market, A buyer showcase is another sort of market that you have to focus on. At the point when the securities exchange, every single together, begins to experience a bigger time of expanding stock costs, at that point you are in a bullish market. It is feasible for the entire market to be bullish and for a solitary stock to be bullish also. Offer The offer will be the measure of cash that you as a dealer are eager to pay for each portion of a stock or another security that you need to work with. It will need to adjust itself against the picked ask cost. This is the sum that a vendor needs for each portion of a similar stock or security. The spread will be significant also because the distinction appears between the asking cost and the offer. Influence One of the things that you can utilize when you are exchanging alternatives is influence. At the point when you choose to utilize influence when you exchange, you will acquire the offers in stock from the representative. The objective of doing this is to assist you with seeing an expansion in the measure of benefit that you can take in.

On the off chance that you can acquire offers and, at that point sell them just for a more significant expense, later on, you would then be able to restore the offers to the specialist and keep any distinction. Be that as it may, if things turn out badly, it can truly put your cash and your record in danger, so it is frequently a risky game to play when you are a learner.

Edge An edge account is going to let you acquire some cash, or apply for a new line of credit, from your merchant. You will at that point utilize this to buy the speculation that you need. The distinction that appears between the measure

of the credit, and the value that you pay for the protections, will be known as the edge. Exchanging on the edge can be an unsafe game to play, particularly on the off chance that you are a tenderfoot. If you are ineffective with your exchanges, at that point you will miss out on a great deal of cash.

You additionally need to have a base parity of capital in your edge account before the representative will consider doing this with you.

Portfolio The arrangement of a speculator will be the entire assortment of ventures that they own. You can have only one stock or security in your portfolio. In any case, numerous effective brokers have developed to having loads of various protections in their portfolio simultaneously This assists with constraining the measure of hazard that they are managing and makes it simpler for them to make more benefits all the while. Short undercutting When you choose to sell one of your protections, it implies that you will get shares from someone else, with the guarantee of returning them to that individual, ordinarily, your dealer, at a settled upon a point not far off. You are then expecting to sell that alternative, and its fundamental resource, for a benefit. This is an extraordinary route for you to exploit any choice and fundamental resource that you believe is going to diminish in cost sooner rather than later. After you undercut them, you are then ready to utilize the benefits to buy the offers at a lower value point.

The distinction that you get from the deal will be your cost as a benefit. This is an incredible move to make when you are working with an unstable market and when you realize how to peruse the various examples that will occur in the market. Simply ensure that you represent the various expenses and commissions that your dealer will charge for acquiring the protections, and guarantee that you are sure the market will go down and you will have the option to make a benefit on these simultaneously.

Spread another term that we have to think about is the spread. This will be the distinction that appears between the offer and the asking cost. This can likewise be viewed as the contrast between the sum that somebody will spend to get security and the sum that another person is happy to sell that equivalent security. Along these lines, if the broker will buy the choice for $10, however, the merchant needs to get $12, at that point the spread will be $2. A considered choice A call will be the choice agreement that gives the broker the right, yet they don't have any commitment, to buy a predetermined measure of the security that is connected to the alternative, normally a bond or a stock, at a predefined cost either during or on the termination date. The cost will be known as the strike cost, and afterward, the timeframe is the sale. If you are hoping to buy a choice that gives you the option to buy explicit security later on, at that point you are working with a call alternative.

On the off chance that the market carries on in the manner that you might want, at that point you can practice your right, either previously or at the termination date, to buy them at the predetermined value, paying little heed to what the market estimation of them is around then. In any case, if the the market doesn't go the way that you need, you can leave and simply surrender the top-notch that you paid in the first place. A put alternative is an inverse of what we saw with a call choice. This one is going to give the proprietor the right, however no commitment, to sell a predetermined measure of a security at a predefined cost inside a specific time. It resembles a security strategy on your portfolio and can guarantee that you downplay your misfortunes. The key takeaways to recall with the put choice incorporates: These permit you to sell fundamental security under specific terms. You need to do it by the termination date, in any case, the alternatives contract terms won't be substantial.

Put alternatives can be utilized with bunches of various resources.

This incorporates things like monetary standards, items, lists, and stocks. The costs of these put alternatives will be influenced by the cost of the fundamental resource, just as time rot.

Time rot will be extremely significant with regards to alternatives and a large number of the methodologies that you decide to work with. This should be viewed as when you are pondering the likely benefit and should take as much weight as the commissions and the charges that are surveyed by your intermediary.

Time rot will be the tendency that your alternatives are going to diminish in complete worth as they draw nearer and closer to their lapse date. The degree of the time rot will be contrarily associated with the variability of that choice. It essentially implies that if you need to sit tight for the right to the termination date of the alternative, at that point it is consequently going to be worth not exactly previously, and you may not make as much benefit as in the past. Alternatives are viewed as squandering resources and they are going to see misfortune in esteem the more you have them.

CHAPTER 5:

Understanding the Basic Techniques

Technical analysis

Entering a trade is as much about knowing how to use your platform as it is about knowing how to validate and time trades so that you can maximize your profitability from each trade that you enter. Every expert trader knows that no trade should ever be entered before appropriate technical analysis has been conducted to ensure that you are entering trades that are likely to earn you profits. Even though the stock market may seem like a gamble because your results are never guaranteed, you should never approach the stock market with a gambling mentality. Every single move that you make should always be purposeful and well-educated to minimize your risk and possible losses while also maximizing your profits and possible income.

Technical analysis is part of research and facts, and part of confidence and intuition. You must learn about how you can leverage both facts and intuition to create strong trade moves that will help you maximize your profits in trading. Without the right research and logical foundation, your trades will always be a gamble.

Likewise, without the right confidence and intuitive belief that the position you are making is correct, each trade will be volatile. Your research helps guarantee the quality of your position, while your confidence helps guarantee the quality of your state of mind upon entering any trade.

Technical Indicators You Need to Know About

When it comes to technical indicators for trading options, there are three indicators that you need to know about to help you make your trades. These indicators are used to help you identify stock trends and patterns so that you can get a strong understanding of what the stocks are doing and where your best positions are going to be.

You should always check technical indicators as a part of your technical analysis to ensure that the position you are taking is going to earn you the best income possible.

The three technical indicators that you need to know about include the relative strength index indicator (RSI), the moving average convergence divergence indicator (MACD), and the stochastic indicator.

Each of these will let you know what is going on with any particular stock and whether or not that stock offers a good position for you to trade-in.

Relative Strength Index (RSI)

The relative strength index is a momentum indicator that sits on a separate scale from the candlestick chart that you will be looking at when you look at the stock market for any given stock value.

The indicator is shown as a single line that is scaled from 0 to 100 and it identifies any stocks that have been overbought or oversold, meaning that you will identify which stocks are due for a rebound in the coming days.

On the indicator, which is shown on the side of the screen, you will notice that there are two white "frames" on either side of it, each of which shows where the market is peaking at overbought or oversold. The top frame represents stocks that have risen over 70 on the indicator, which indicates the market has been overbought and people are about to start selling their shares to earn profits before the market switches in the opposite direction.

The bottom frame represents stocks that have dropped below 30 on the indicator, indicating that the market has been oversold and people are about to start buying those stocks.

You can watch for trends in any given stock on the RSI to see how they tend to perform and where they are presently sitting based on the intensity of trades that have been happening with that particular stock.

Most stocks will not consistently swing back and forth between overbought and oversold but instead will straddle one side of the indicator before taking a large swing into the opposite direction at any given point in the future.

With that being said, you should always take your time spotting trends on this indicator so that you can confirm the trend is happening. Although this will eat into some of your profits, it will still help you ensure that you are earning plenty from the trade that you are seeking to make.

Moving Average Convergence Divergence (MACD)

The MACD indicator shows a fast line, a slow line, and a histogram that is used to help identify what is taking place with any given stock. This particular indicator can be more challenging to understand, but it still offers a wealth of valuable knowledge that will help you identify how the stock is behaving.

You should take your time to understand the MACD and educate yourself by watching it on the active stock market screen so that you can get a feel for the information it provides

you with. Once you understand how to read this indicator, you will find a great deal of information that helps reinforce your trade decisions going forward.

The MACD indicator shows the moving average of the difference between the fast line and the slow line on the indicator itself. This means that what you are reading is how quickly the market is moving back and forth, or how volatile the market is with any given stock at any given moment.

The MACD slow line shows you the moving average of the last line over several periods defined as "MA-periods."

The MACD indicator is shown by two lines with the last line being represented by the color blue and the slow line being represented by the color orange. The bigger the gap is between the two lines, the more volatile the market is. When the two lines cross, it shows that the market has switched in trend, resulting in it either turning bullish or bearish from a bearish or bullish trend, depending on what direction it moves into. The histogram shows you the moving average of the stock so that you can get a feel for how volatile the stock has been in the past, allowing you to understand whether or not the current volatility of the stock is standard or unusual for that particular stock. If it is standard, you know that the patterns of the stock will more than likely follow patterns similar to the ones it has in the past.

In other words, this is considered a lower-risk stock investment. If the indicator suggests that the stock is more volatile, this means that it is less likely to follow historical patterns and that it will likely perform more unpredictably.

In other words, the stock is riskier and could come with greater losses. With that being said, higher-risk stocks do generally offer higher rewards, too, meaning it may be worth the risk depending on how confident you are in your judgment of how the stock will truly behave.

Stochastic Indicator

The stochastic indicator is a momentum indicator that can
help you identify when a trend might end, letting you know
when a stock has either been overbought or oversold. The
information given by the stochastic indicator is similar to
what you receive from an RSI, meaning that it can help
validate whether or not the trade position you are looking at
is ideal.

The stochastic indicator is shown by two lines on a chart that
is separate from the candlestick chart that represents the
market itself. Typically, it is shown below the market chart
and follows the same timestamps, meaning that the
information you see in the stochastic indicator chart perfectly
overlaps with the information you see in the market itself.

The stochastic indicator looks almost exactly like the RSI, with

a frame on each the top and bottom of the chart itself showing
you the overbought and oversold portions of the market
respectively.

However, the stochastic indicator has two lines, a red and a
blue line, moving through the chart to give you information
about what is currently going on in the marketplace.

When the lines are above the "80" point, this means a downtrend is likely to follow, or the market is likely to go bearish. In this case, you would want to sell your call options or buy your put options, depending on what strategy you are using to earn your profits from the market.

If it drops below the "20" point, the market has been oversold and it is going to turn into an uptrend or a bullish market. This is where you would want to buy your call options, sell your put options, or otherwise position yourself with the best spread and strategy to earn profits from the incoming movement of the stock prices.

When reading the stochastic indicator, you want to see both lines rise above 80 or fall below 20 to indicate that there is a strong chance for the market to switch directions. If only one-line crosses, this suggests that the market may be reaching overbought or oversold, but it has not reached it yet and therefore it is not yet ready to swing back into the opposite direction.

Pay close attention to these stocks, however, as they will likely mature into their overbought or oversold position quickly, leading to an opportunity for you to secure an entry into the market.

Technical Analysis for Evaluating a Trade

Options trading requires less technical analysis than other trade styles, but you are still required to perform technical analysis to ensure that the market entry point you are looking at is going to be profitable. Entering any market at any time without having first completed proper technical analysis can lead to a greater risk of losses due to not clearly understanding what is likely going to happen with the market in its current state.

When you perform technical analysis, your goal is to identify possible positions that you can enter, validate the quality of those positions, choose the position(s) you will take, and then pick the perfect entry point. By following this exact system for entering the market, you can feel confident that you are entering the market at the best possible time, every single time. This way, you maximize your potential for profits and minimize your potential for losses.

Remember, the more educated you are on what you are doing and what position you are taking, the more likely you are

going to be able to increase your profits with trading. Conducting technical analysis for options trading should be completed as a routine every time you do it to ensure that you never miss out on a step. This way, you create a strong system that works for validating your positions and you can always feel confident that you are taking on the best positions possible.

CHAPTER 6:

Learn to Become a Day Trader

The popularity of day trading started in the late 1990s, during the Dot-com bubble. For day traders, it was easy to book profits during those days; they did not need any skill. The stock markets used to make such big moments that it became easy to buy and sell internet stocks and make huge profits every day. That was a brief, but the very heady and profitable period for day traders, as they traded tech company stocks and made big money. The tech index NASDAQ was skyrocketing during that time, going up by thousands of points within a few months. Day trading was a booming business because it was a huge wave in the tech ocean, and traders were surfing on the back of that wave. Once the Dot-com bubble burst and markets came back to their normal trading pattern, day trading also became less profitable. However; it remained a lucrative career for many people.

With the Dot-com era, online trading also saw rapid expansion. That brought day trading within reach of common people. It made people realize, day trading was also a profession, like other professions, where one can achieve success with mastering the required knowledge and skill set. In day trading, one buys and sells stocks, or any other financial entity, through the day. For doing so they need to know various skills and tools, understand the right time to buy or sell stocks. Big financial companies cropped up overnight and started day trading on behalf of their clients. Banking institutions started opening their securities branches for common people, where they trained their clients to become skilled in trading.

Since then, the popularity of day trading as an income-producing vocation has been increasing. If you are looking to become a successful day trader, here are a few things that you will need to learn:

Knowledge about stock markets: As a day trader, have at least a basic knowledge of stock markets. You should know which stocks or companies are popular in the stock market. They will trade with higher volume, and volumes play an important part in day trading.

Basic principles of technical analysis: Unlike the fundamental analysis, the technical analysis tells how the price will move in a smaller timeframe, which is essential knowledge for a day traders. So, if you are thinking about making day trading your career, this is a skill set that you must have. There are many online courses in technical analysis and chart reading. Various institutions also conduct offline workshops to teach this. You can join any of them and gain a basic knowledge of how to analyze charts, and what tools to use for day trading.

Money management skills: This goes without saying that you cannot spend an unlimited amount of money on stock trading. Before you start, you must set aside a fixed amount for your trading business and manage that money carefully. You should always know your losses and profits so you will understand how your trading business is going: successfully or failing miserably. You can find many books online about money management in day trading. Reading a few popular ones will give you a good idea of how to manage your risk and reward ratio.

Learn about trading psychology: Emotions are terrible for day trading, and you must have some knowledge about controlling your emotions during trading. Many successful day traders have written books about trading psychology. It will be a good idea to read a few of them before you trade.

No business can survive on emotion, and before you enter the trading arena, you should be able to control your emotions; whether you make profits and losses.

What Differentiates a Day Trader?

Day traders are technical traders. They rely on chart readings for executing their trades and ignore any other thing like the company's profitability, P/E ratio, debt-to-equity ratio, etc. For a day trader, technical charts are the only tools for making money. Usually, day traders trade through a single session, and by the close of the day, they also close all open trades, not keeping any position open for the next day. Traders who keep their position open for the next session or overnight, are swing traders.

A day trader can use many time frames on technical charts for trading. These time frames can range from one minute or lower to 5 minutes; 15 minutes; 30 minutes; 45 minutes; 1 hour; 4 hours; or even weekly and monthly. If you are wondering how day traders can use weekly or monthly charts, know the difference between using various time frames. Day traders decide their trading style by looking at the charts and deciding which time frame will suit them the most. Many day traders can spend hours in front of their computer screens every day. But several day traders trade only part-time, are busy with other jobs or work, and cannot spend much time trading every day. In such situations, these traders can study weekly or monthly charts, and decide at what price a level they will buy or sell any stock. After deciding that, they wait patiently for that level to arrive and trade only at then. There are many ways to set an alert to know when a price level has reached. The brokerage platforms have SMS facilities to alert their clients about stock prices. Mostly, charting software also has facilities to alert about a stock price level. By trading this way, they save precious time and money, which they can use for pursuing other money-making activities like a regular job or doing some other work.

There is another. highly skilled type of day trading, call scalping. This is also known as micro-trading because the day trader focuses on a small timeframe (such as one minute or a few seconds), and trades for tiny profits. They keep the lot sizes higher so that small profits will also multiply into big money. Since the timeframe is very small, scalpers can trade several times throughout the day, sometimes even 20 to 50 times. But this is a risky type of trading and requires very fine trading skills. Otherwise; one can end up losing all the trading money within a single session.

Day trading is also about buying and selling on the same day. But compared to scalping, day traders have a bigger time frame for keeping their positions open. This can range from minutes to hours. The Internet is full of articles that portray glamorous pictures of day trading, making you believe that you can get rich quickly by this trading method.

But this trading method requires hard work, knowledge, razor-sharp focus, and high levels of patience; not to mention a big chunk of money to invest in the early stages. If you are day trading, then you should be completely focused, you cannot allow yourself to be distracted by other things. If you can afford to have this kind of discipline and dedication, then you will find day trading suits you.

Another name for day trading is intraday trading. This term is a clearer definition of a day trader since it shows that buying and selling are happening within one day.

Day traders can develop their style into other types of trading such as momentum trading, positional trading, swing trading, or long-term trading. All these styles are specialization forms of trading, but usually, do not fall under the day trading category.

Part-Time, or Full-Time Day Trading?

For day trading you do not have to stay glued to your computer screen throughout the day. You can do part-time day trading or full-time.

As a full-time day trader, the best option will be to join any big financial institution as a day trader and work for them. This will ensure that you get a monthly salary, and perks, if you're performing well. This will suit you if you think of day trading as a hobby and do not wish to put your money at risk by trading. You will also benefit from the company's trading recommendations that are regularly sent to their clients. You can utilize them for your trading while doing the job.

On the other hand, you can opt to be a full-time individual day trader. Here you will have to do all your setup, invest your own money and rely on your skills and knowledge.

As an individual trader, you can also adopt a part-time trading routine, if you do not wish to let go of your stable job and jump into full-time day trading. All you have to do, is observe markets, find out which hours have a higher level of trading activity (or higher volumes), then trade only during those hours. For example, if you are looking for day trading in stock options and futures, the highest trading activity in

these entities happen at the opening and closing hours of the stock market. Just prepare your trading strategies, and plan how you will trade (buy or sell). After that, you can trade only in the first hour of markets' opening, or the last hour of markets' closing. The price volatility is very high during these hours because big traders are opening or closing their positions and preparing for the next day. This makes the price move constantly and gives day traders a good chance to earn profits within that hour. Remember, the volatility levels will be very high during these hours, and you must be highly skilled and emotionally stable to tackle trading during this time frame. If you let emotions like fear and greed overpower you during these trading hours; chances are you will end up making wrong trades and suffering losses.

For those, who cannot day trade during the regular hours in stock markets, forex markets provide an excellent chance of trading through the 24 hours. Forex or currency markets function Monday to Friday, 24 hours a day, and close only on the weekend. This gives day traders unlimited access to trading through the week, and they can trade at the time most convenient for them. Because of this, forex trading is more popular than stock trading among day traders. Another thing that favors forex trading is the very technical nature of this trading. Anybody who has a basic knowledge of technical analysis, can trade in forex markets and be successful.

There are different currency pairs that day traders can pick for trading.

In forex markets also, the opening times of major regional markets provide higher levels of activity, which day traders can take advantage of. First among such active times is the opening in Asia markets, then the opening time of European stock markets, and the highest level of activity in forex markets is seen when the US stock markets open. So, one can also become a part-time or full-time day trader in forex markets. For trading in forex markets, learning technical analysis is necessary. Knowing the schedule of important economic events is also essential because these events usually trigger extreme volatility in forex markets.

CHAPTER 7:

Fundamental Analysis

Fundamental analysis is more realistic and feasible in the long term. The whole premise behind the fundamental analysis is that you look at the economy of the country and the trading system that's going on to determine whether it is a good trade or not. More focusing on economics, that's why it helps you to figure out which dollar is going up or down and what is causing it.

One of the greatest things you can do when it comes to Options Trading is to understand why a dollar is dropping or going up. Once you're able to understand that, you will be in a much better position for gaining profits in your Option Trading endeavors. When using the fundamental analysis, you will be looking at the country's employment and unemployment rate also sees how the training with different countries overall sing the country's economy before you decide on whether you should try it or not. Many successful

Option Traders solely believe in fundamental analysis, as it is factual, unlike technical analysis. Even though technical analysis is accurate, it is not guaranteed like the theoretical analysis. Instead of looking at the trends, you will be looking at what is causing the highs and the lows. Not only that, based on the highs and lows, you will be able to determine the country's current and future economic outlook, whether it is good or not. One rule of thumb to look into with be how good the country is doing, the better the country is doing, the more foreign investors are going to take part in it. Once starting the piece in it, the dollar or the stock in that country will go up tremendously.

 The idea behind fundamental analysis is that you need to look at the countries economically and you also need to look at them. To make you understand, what fundamental analysis is it is mostly when you invest in a country that is doing good in the economy, and not invest in a company when they're doing bad in the marketplace. Which makes sense since the economy dictates how high are low prices going to be per dollar. Most of the time, investors will invest the money as soon as they see the dollar going up. The reason why they will do that is that they know the dollar will keep climbing up since the economy is getting better. One of the great examples would be when the US dollar dropped in 2007 2008, and the

The Canadian dollar took up, at that point, a lot of investors are investing in Canadian dollars of the US dollar. After a very long time, the US dollar was dropping tremendously, whereas the Canadian dollar was more expensive than the US dollar. This was one of the anomalies which took place back in the day. If you were to use technical analysis in this instance, then you will not get a lot of success out of this economic drop. This is why fundamental analysis could work a lot better for most people in the long-term and in the short-term, which is why many top traders recommend you follow fundamental analysis instead of technical analysis to find out which dollar you're going to be investing in.

Which Method to Use and When?

Now we get into the part where we show you which method to use and when ideally what Options Trading you would like to dabble with technical analysis and fundamental analysis to see optimal success. However, you can do fundamental analysis and see progress, both long-term and short-term. In our opinion the best way to go about it would be to try out technical analysis in the short-term, the reason why we think the technical analysis, in short, would work very good for you is that it is something that you can't go wrong with if you do it properly. As we explained to you what technical analysis is, you can see why it is so good for someone to start with technical analysis and to see amazing results out of it. Another thing technical analysis can help you out with would be that it will help you to build up your confidence in the beginning. When you're starting Option Trading especially in the beginning, you must build up confidence and you make yourself believe that you can, make money from Options Trading.

This will help you to continue with your Options Trading journey and to learn more, more accurately help you to start investing your money the right way, and to continue off becoming a full-time Option Trader. Once you have dabbled with technical analysis, you can start doing your more long-term trades with fundamental analysis. The only problem with fundamental analysis would be that there's a lot more research to be done, and if you're trying to make Options Trading a long-term income Source or a full-time income Source, then the chances are you should be doing your research before you make a trade. Keep in mind that, fundamental analysis will help you to keep going in the long-term and will yield you the best results possible. Even though technical analysis has a higher success rate, fundamental analysis will be a lot more long-term. Secondly, the more you do fundamental analysis, the easier it's going to get for you. Keeping that in mind, the best method to go about Options Trading, in the beginning, would be to start with technical analysis make small trades, and make some money. This will help you to build up your confidence with Options Trading and therefore, help you to keep going on. The second thing you should be doing is research on the fundamental analysis I'm slowly started dabbling with it until you are sure on which dollar or stock on investing based on your research. You will require some brainpower to dabble with Options Trading using fundamental analysis. However, once you understand it and start dabbling with it, you will see the success they are looking for with Options Trading. The final the verdict would be to use both of them however used technical analysis, in the beginning, to really see some short-term benefits out of it and then eventually branch off to fundamental analysis and then dabbing our technical analysis trading there to see the small incremental games. When combined both you will be in a much better position to make a lot of money from Options Trading.

Fundamental Analysis Rules

The best time to use fundamental analysis is when you are looking to gain a broad idea of the state of the market as it stands and how that relates to the state of things shortly when it comes time to trading successfully. Regardless of what market you are considering, the end goals are the same, find the most effective trade for the period that you are targeting. Establish a baseline: To begin analyzing the fundamentals, the first thing that you will need to do is to create a baseline regarding the company's overall performance. To generate the most useful results possible, the first thing that you are going to need to do is to gather data both regarding the company in question as well as the related industry as a whole. When gathering macro data, it is important to keep in mind that no market is going to operate in a vacuum which means the reasons behind specific market movement can be much more far-reaching than they first appear. Fundamental analysis works because of the stock market's propensity for patterns which means if you trace a specific market moved back to the source you will have a better idea of what to keep an eye on in the future.

Furthermore, all industries go through several different phases where their penny stocks are going to be worth more or less overall based on general popularity. If the industry is producing many popular penny stocks, then overall volatility will be down while at the same time liquidity will be at an overall high. Consider worldwide issues: Once you have a general grasp on the current phase you are dealing with, the next thing you will want to consider is anything that is going on in the wider world that will after the type of businesses you tend to favor in your penny stocks. Not being prepared for major paradigm shifts, especially in penny stocks where new companies come and go so quickly, means that you can easily miss out on massive profits and should be avoided at all costs. To ensure you are not blindsided by news you could have seen coming, it is important to look beyond the obvious issues that are consuming the 24-hour news cycle and dig deeper into the comings and goings of the nations that are going to most directly affect your particular subsection of penny stocks. One important worldwide phenomenon that you will want to pay specific attention to is anything in the realm of technology as major paradigm shifts like the adoption of the smartphone, or the current move towards electric cars can create serious paradigm shifts.

Put it all together:

Once you have a clear idea of what the market should look like as well as what may be on the horizon, the next step is to put it all together to compare what has been and what might to what the current state of the market is. Not only will this give you a realistic idea of what other investors are going to do if certain events occur the way they have in the past, you will also be able to use these details to identify underlying assets that are currently on the cusp of generating the type of movement that you need if you want to utilize them via binary options trades. The best time to get on board with a new underlying asset is when it is nearing the end of the post-bust period or the end of a post-boom period depending on if you are going to place a call or a put. In these scenarios, you are going to have the greatest access to the freedom of the market and thus have access to the greatest overall allowable risk that you are going to find in any market. Remember, the amount of risk that you can successfully handle without an increase in the likelihood of failure is going to start decreasing as soon as the boom or bust phase begins in earnest so it is important to get in as quickly as possible if you hope to truly maximize your profits. Understand the relative strength of any given trade.

CHAPTER 8:

Technical Analysis for Training Options

When working with technical analysis you are always going to want to remember that it functions because of the belief that the way the price of a given trade has moved in the past is going to be an equally reliable metric for determining what it is likely to do again in the future. Regardless of which market you choose to focus on, you'll find that there is always more technical data available than you will ever be able to realistically parse without quite a significant amount of help. Luckily, you won't be sifting through the data all on your own, and you will have numerous technical tools including things such as charts, trends, and indicators to help you push your success rates to new heights.

While some of the methods you will be asked to apply might

seem arcane at first, the fact of the matter is that all you are essentially doing is looking to determine future trends along with their relative strengths. This, in turn, is crucial to your long-term success and will make each of your trades more reliable practically every single time.

Understand core assumptions: Technical analysis is all about measuring the relative value of a particular trade or underlying asset by using available tools to find otherwise invisible patterns that, ideally, few other people have currently noticed. When it comes to using technical analysis properly you are going to always need to assume three things are true. First and foremost, the market ultimately discounts everything; second, trends will always be an adequate predictor of price and third, history is bound to repeat itself when given enough time to do so.

Technical analysis believes that the current price of the underlying asset in question is the only metric that matters when it comes to looking into the current state of things outside of the market, specifically because everything else is already automatically factored in when the current price is set as it is. As such, to accurately use this type of analysis all you need to know is the current price of the potential trade-in question as well as the greater economic climate as a whole. Those who practice technical analysis are then able to interpret what the price is suggesting about market sentiment

Price charts

to make predictions about where the price of a given cryptocurrency is going to go in the future. This is possible because pricing movements aren't random. Instead, they follow trends that appear in both the short and the long-term. Determining these trends in advance is key to using technical analysis successfully because all trends are likely to repeat themselves over time, thus the use of historical charts to determine likely trends in the future.

When it comes to technical analysis, what is always going to be more important than the why. That is, the fact that the price

moved in a specific way is far more important to a technical analyst than why it made that particular movement. Supply and demand should always be consulted, but beyond that, there are likely too many variables to make it worthwhile to consider all of them as opposed to their results.

Technical analysis is all about the price chart which is a chart with an x and y-axis. The price is measured along the vertical axis and the time is measured via the horizontal axis. There are numerous different types of price charts that different types of traders prefer, these include the point and figure chart, the Reno chart, the Kagin chart, the Heikin-Ashi chart, the bar chart, the candlestick chart, the line chart, and the tick chart. However, the ones you will need to concern yourself with at first are going to be included in any forex trading platform software and are the bar chart, the candlestick chart, the line chart, and the point and click chart which is why they are outlined in greater detail below.

Line chart: Of all the various types of charts, the line charts are

the simplest because it only presents price information in the form of closing prices in a fixed time. The lines that give it its name is created when the various closing price points are then connected with a line. When looking at a line chart it is important to keep in mind that they will not be able to provide an accurate visual representation of the range that individual points reached which means you won't be able to see either opening prices or those that were high or low before close. Regardless, the closing point is important to always consider which is why this chart is so commonly referred to by technical traders of all skill levels.

Bar chart: A bar chart takes the information that can be found in a line chart and expands upon it in several interesting ways. For starters, the chart is made using several vertical lines that provide information on various data points. The top and bottom of the line can then be thought of as the high and low of the trading timeframe respectively while the closing price is also indicated with a dash on the right side of the bar. Furthermore, the point where the currency price opened is indicated via a dash and will show up on the left side of the bar in question.

Candlestick chart: A candlestick chart is similar to a bar chart, though the information it provides is much more detailed overall. Like a bar chart it includes a line to indicate the range for the day, however, when you are looking at a candlestick chart you will notice a wide bar near the vertical line which indicates the degree of the difference the price saw throughout the day. If the price that the stock is trading at increases overall for the day, then the candlestick will often be clear while if the price has decreased then the candlestick is going to be read.

Point and figure chart: While seen less frequently than some of the other types of charts, a point and figure chart has been around for nearly a century and can still be useful in certain situations today. This chart can accurately reflect the way the price is going to move, though it won't indicate timing or volume. It can be thought of as a pure indicator of price with the excessive noise surrounding the market muted, ensuring nothing is skewed.

A point and figure chart are noticeable because it is made up of Xs and Os rather than lines and points. The Xs will indicate points where positive trends occurred while the Os will indicate periods of downward movement. You will also notice numbers and letters listed along the bottom of the chart which corresponds to months as well as dates. This type of chart will also make it clear how much the price is going to have to move for an X to become an O or an O to become an X.

Trend or range: When it comes to using technical analysis successfully, you will want to determine early on if you are more interested in trading based on the trends you find or on the range. While they are both properties related to price, these two concepts are very different in practice which means you will want to choose one to emphasize over the other.

Chart Patterns to Be Aware Of Flags and Pennants: Both flags and pennants show retracement, which is deviations that will be visible in the short term about the primary trend.

Retracement results in no breakout occurring from either the resistance or support levels but this won't matter as the security will also not be following the dominant trend.

Head Above Shoulders Formation: If you are looking for indicators of how long any one particular trend is likely to continue, then looking for a grouping of three peaks in a price chart, known as the head above shoulders formation, can indicate a bearish pattern moving forward. The peaks to the left and the right of the primary peak, also known as the shoulders, should be somewhat smaller than the head peak and also connect at a specific price. This price is known as the neckline and when it reaches the right shoulder the price will likely then plunge noticeably.

The head and shoulders top form at the peaks of an upwards trend and signals that a reversal is often forthcoming through a process of four steps. The first of these starts with the creation of the far-left shoulder which can be formed when the cryptocurrency reaches a new high before dropping to a new low. This is then followed by the formation of the head which occurs when the security reaches an even higher high before retracing back to the low found in the left shoulder. Finally, the right shoulder is formed from a high that is lower than the high found in the head, countered by a retracement back to the low of the left shoulder. The pattern is then completed when the price drops back below the neckline.

In both instances, the price dipping below the neckline signals the true reversal of the trend in question which means the security will now be moving in the opposite direction. This breakout point is often the ideal point to go either short or long depending. It is important to keep in mind, however, that the security is unlikely to continue smoothly in the direction the pattern suggests. As such, you will want to keep an eye out for what is called a throwback move.

Gann: While not universally trusted, Gann indicators have been used by traders for decades and remain a useful way of determining the direction a specific currency is likely to move following. Gann angles are used to determine certain elements of the chart include price, time, and pattern which makes it easier to determine the future, past, and even present of the market as well as how that information will determine the future of the price.

While you could be forgiven for thinking they are similar to trend lines, Gann's angles are a different beast entirely.

They are, in fact, a series of diagonal lines that move at a fixed rate and can likely be generated by your trading program. When they are compared to a trend line you will notice the Gann angle makes it possible for users to determine a true price at a specific point in the future assuming the current trend continues at its current strength.

CHAPTER 9:

How to Find the Best Options to Get Started

Having the right mindset is so much important if you want to be a successful trader. It can be a game-changer. Like I already told you before, options are truly one of the most versatile instruments in the financial world. You simply have to learn how you can use them to your benefit, and one of the skills that you have to learn in the process is how you can acquire the mindset of an options trader.

Strategies to Think Like an Option Trader

Let me tell you about a little secret, which is not that much of a secret after all. If you truly want to become a successful trader, you should not only be excelling at figuring out the best strategies, but you should also be having a winning mindset. An extensive analysis can help you get your facts straight but when you are trading, your mindset can play a huge role. It is not the trading strategies or perfect market analysis or simple smartness that helps you win trades, but it is your psychological mindset that will get you a long way.

Most of the beginners with whom I have interacted have always told me the same thing – they are trying to figure out the right strategy, and they usually remain quite stressed about doing so. Most beginners think that once you have the best strategy, all you have to do is apply it and money will come rushing into your bank account. But that's not what happens.

Once you are in the trading world for quite some time, you will understand that trading is not all about strategies and numbers, and sometimes, it can even be tough. There are so many traders just like you who are waiting for their golden opportunity to become a millionaire, and they are all intelligent and well-learned. They even have designed full-proof strategies which are doubt solid. But you will notice that even they end up losing money from time to time.

On the other hand, some traders can show you a record of consistent wins, and do you know the secret behind their consistency? It is their psychological mindset. Trading psychology is a thing, believe it or not, and it is heavily researched too. There are several psychological characteristics, mindsets, attitudes, and beliefs that are studied under that system, and you have to know them too if you want to make it big in the trading world.

Some of the most common beliefs and attitudes about the market include you thinking that the market is rigged against you. But that is only a false belief that you have to breakthrough.

It is erroneous and can put you in a negative state of mind. If you keep thinking like that, you won't be able to pull off your trades successfully. No one in the

market is trying to go behind your back, and if you think so, then you simply have to change your perspective and look at it differently. If you continue to delve yourself into such baseless thoughts, then you will not be able to make a correct evaluation of the opportunities that arise in the market. Remember one thing very clearly – the market is not biased at all.

It is neutral, and there is not a shred of doubt about that. The market does not care whether you are losing all your money or winning loads.

Your trading psychology is responsible for the beliefs that you have, and these beliefs can get so deeply rooted in your subconscious that sometimes they can push you into a toxic cycle of self-doubt.

If you analyze the mentalities of traders who have lost successively, you will notice that one thing is common with most of them, and that is – there is this nagging self-doubt that brings all the negativity in their life. You have to realize that you are walking on the path of a self-fulfilling prophecy if you think that you have bad luck and so you cannot win. You will have difficulty initiating trades at the right time or implementing strategies at the right time if you doubt your abilities. You will not be able to take the call when you should. This can not only reduce your profits but can also create negative income.

On the other hand, winning traders don't think like that. They know how to respect the conditions of the market, and they know that sometimes, their strategies can mess up, or even if they did everything right, the trade can get messed up and they don't fall into an unnecessary cycle of self-blame. They are confident about themselves and the decisions they make. This confidence is the thing that separates them from losing traders and they never miss a genuine opportunity coming towards them.

Another thing that is consistent with winning traders is that they know when a trade is losing them money and when it is simply a 'bad trade.' You might confuse them both to be the same thing, but they are not. There is a critical difference, and I am going to explain that difference to you right now. Your trade cannot be classified as a bad trade just because you lost some money on it. That trade is a losing trade. The classification of a trade to be good or bad is not judged based on whether you won it or lost it, but what matters is that when compared to the risk, the potential reward is more. Also, regardless of how the trade turns out to be, it will be a good trade if the probabilities or odds are in your favor. So, once you have taken a trade, if you are managing well with it no matter whether you win money or lose it, it will still be a good trade.

Similarly, if we are to think of the converse, even if you won money from trade, but the risk to reward ratio was bad, or if it was not initiated on good terms then no matter how much profit you made, that trade will still be considered to be bad. Trading is quite a demanding task, and many people fail to understand that before jumping right into it. When you have a predetermined direction set in your mind, and the trade does not go your way, you will be facing a myriad of emotions, and the same applies to the scenario when the trade, does go in your direction. And thus, trades often face an adrenaline rush, which, in turn, leads to a threatening, dangerous, and stressful situation. No matter how calm and composed you are in your life, when you enter the trading floor, maintaining that same demeanor is quite a tough task. The stress and the pressure that you will be experiencing are something that you haven't before.

To truly think like an options trader, you have to learn how to think in probabilities. Yes, when it is your hard-earned money that is on the line, it might be a bit difficult to think in this way, but you simply have to learn it. Let us say that a particular strategy says that when applied to a bunch of trades, it will give you a 50-50 ratio of win/lose. So, even when you have this data in hand and have a full-proof risk management strategy along with a trading plan in hand, what else can you do? Nothing, because you have to follow your trading plan.

In short, you should not be feeling too elated on a winning trade, neither too depressed on a losing one. This is because, to be a successful options trader, you have to realize that your trades are going to play out only 50% of the time and if you think about anyone trade from the numerous trades you did, that one trade is only a small part of the grand scheme. It will take you some time to develop this attitude and thinking, but you have to keep at it, and only then you will be able to develop the truckloads of discipline you need to be a successful options trader.

Important Traits of a Successful Options Trader

There is a reason that some traders can outperform others, and once you learn about these traits, I hope you will be trying to inculcate those in yourself.

Ability to Manage Risk

You will probably hear everyone say over and over again that proper risk management is what you need to be successful. And traders will not be able to use the risk management strategies if they are not accurate with risk assessment in the first place. Keeping in mind the factor of volatility, you have to understand what an explicit or implicit position is. You also have to assess what the major downside

of trade can be. These are only a few questions that you should be asking yourself. Once the risk is figured out, you have to able to find a way to mitigate the risk or

control it. For example, if you are more into short-term trades in the world of options, there will be plenty of loss-making trades that you will come across in a day. Let us say, you decided to hold your position overnight, and on that same night, some adverse news was released, which completely changed the direction of the market, and so your bet goes bad. But your risk management strategy should be so good that it can control the risk no matter what the situation is.

Diversification is just one of the strategies that traders use to minimize the risks involved in trade, and so their trade size is reduced.

Another trait that you should have to be a successful options trader is that you should be good at managing money. No matter how much capital you have, if you do not manage it wisely, it is ultimately going to go down the drain. One of the very common examples that I can give you is – suppose a trader used 90% of his capital on a single trade and the trade backfires, so he will end up losing almost all his money.

Conclusion

Many years ago, people working for house banking, financial institutions, and brokerages did only regular trading in the stock market. Brokers also simplified matters for the average investor willing to go into trading with the advent of the internet and the rise of online trading houses.

Day trading can be very lucrative if you know how to do it properly, and in the Australian market, it is trendy. Day trading is the buying and selling of an asset during one business day. This method of trading allows you to close all positions at the end of each working day and then continue throughout the day following. Trading on a day is not confined to a single market but is common in stock markets and forex. Day traders buy and sell several commodities in a single day, or even multiple times a day. They use these strategies to take advantage of any price changes in currencies or liquid stocks, no matter how low. You have to be a fast decision-maker as a day trader, and be able to conduct multiple trades every time for a small profit.

Day trading isn't a sport, and can't be. You have to be careful about it and stick to it. Because you need to keep monitoring the open opportunities business trend, you need to have plenty of time during the day to devote to this company.

Be mindful of the market you are on. Try to focus on a few chosen business or financial instruments and focus on them. Over time, you'll be tuned to the market or resources you've decided to focus on. You are going to develop a sixth sense of your market conditions.

The trick is to plan. Always train yourself properly before trading the next day. You still need to do the groundwork necessary; for instance, giving yourself a briefing on how, where, and when you will conduct your trade policy. Having an idea where to put the loss of your stop would make sure you cover your loss point for the day. So you can spend the bulk of the day doing business for profit.

Make sure you stick to your business plan. This will require enormous discipline on your part but is an important part of a successful day trader. There's no easy way to control your greed. This needs a high degree of self-control. Don't try to optimize every single trading point. It is also easier to let go. A winning trade in a fast-changing market can quickly turn into a loss. Often you have to cut a losing role and shouldn't hesitate when the time comes. Taking some small losses is better than waiting for a significant loss to strike you and wipe out your entire wealth.

It's also crucial you never try to capture the market at all. If you miss a good trade for some reason, because you've been late, don't jump in at the latter point. You may be doing it at the high end or low end of the deal by the time you reach the market. Miss the exchange and go back to work the next day. Never engage in a transaction unless you are sure about what you are doing. Do not trade for the merchant's sake or that you are searching for excitement.

To put it another way, do not overtrade. Never trade in trend at the top or bottom end. The market is often dynamic and can go higher or lower than expected. If you're straying from the trend spectrum, you might be on the wrong side of the curve. Protecting your wealth will still be your priority number one. Rentability is secondary to that. Controlling your losses will help ensure you have another day to live to trade. If you keep chasing profits and the market backtracks unexpectedly, you may find that there would be a high proportion of your resources at risk.

Take note of news reports coming up. In particular, keeping an open position before releasing any news, which may influence the market is a bad idea. If you can second-guess the economy, you can never know until the news is released what direction the economy can head in.

CPSIA information can be obtained
at www.ICGtesting.com
Printed in the USA
BVHW042214130421
604819BV00009BA/997